Positive Guidance:

Discipline with *Love*

By Betty Sue Hanks

Copyright © 2004

About the Author

Betty Sue Hanks is a native Texan and the eleventh of thirteen children. She has been in Bryan, Texas for much of her life; she and her husband Melvin have five children, sons Melvin and Derrick, and three daughters, RoShunda, Tanisha and Tashara who are students of the Texas A&M University System.

Hanks received her Bachelor of Science degree from Prairie View A&M in 1965, and her Master of Education Degree from Texas A&M in 1969. She has also participated in additional graduate courses at Texas A&M.

In addition to being a student, Hanks has also been a teacher at many levels. She was a teacher for the Bryan ISD for thirty years, and during that time she supervised and tutored student teachers, was a GED advisor, and made many educational presentations to different audiences. She has been involved in a number of organizations; the Girl Scouts, Texas Education Agency, Bethune Woman's Club, City Mission, Prenatal Clinic, Alpha Kappa Alpha Sorority, and the Children's Museum of the Brazos Valley, just to name a few. Hanks also established scholarships for two high school students, and a similar program exists for her employees as well.

Another of Hanks' achievements is the Big Top Learning Center. She has been the owner and director of the center for 22 years, and it is a nationally accredited center. This means that Hanks and her staff went through the voluntary process of becoming accredited through the National Association for the Education of Young Children to demonstrate that their program met the national standards of excellence. In addition to providing excellent child care and education to its patrons, the center also is a place for college students majoring in this area to come and learn about their field.

The Mayor of Bryan declared March 6 as "Big Top Learning Center Day" for the accomplishments of the center. In 2001 Hanks was named "Administrator of the Year of the Brazos Valley Association for the Education of Young Children," and she is listed in the 2002 "Who's Who National Register" as an Honored Professional for Executives and Business. Hanks is also a validator for the National Association for the Education of Young Children.

About the Author

Other books by the author:

Early Childhood Curriculum Book (ages birth-12 months)
Early Childhood Curriculum Resource Book (ages birth-12 months)

Copyright © 2004 by Betty Hanks
First Edition Printing

For additional Copies write to:
Betty Hanks
Life Long Learning
906 Dansby
Bryan, Texas 77803
website: www.rmbhanks.com

No part of this book may be reproduced by any means without the written permission of the author.

Cover Illustration by Jean Benavides (jini0112@comcast.net)
Book Design and Typesetting by Just Your Type Desktop Publishing, San Antonio, TX (210) 599-8121
Edited by Amber M. Malinovsky (Amalinov03@aol.com)
Published by Life Long Learning, Bryan, TX

Acknowledgments

The author wishes to acknowledge with great gratitude the patience and encouragement of her husband, Melvin Hanks, and her children RoShunda, Tanisha, and Tashara Hanks.

Dedication

*Dedicated to
my daughters,
RoShunda,
Tanisha,
and
Tashara Hanks*

Table of Contents

I.	Foreword	viii
II.	Introduction	ix
III.	Discipline	2
IV.	Why Children Misbehave	4
V.	Some Suggested Strategies for Preventing Misbehavior	8
VI.	Positive Guidance Approach	10
VII.	What Teachers Can Do	16
VIII.	Teaches' Responsibility for Discipline	22
IX.	What Children Should Know	24
X.	What Parents Can Do	26
XI.	Guiding Children in Solving Conflicts	32
XII.	Discipline Methods	36
XIII.	Keys to Positive Discipline	42
XIV.	Conclusion	44
XV.	Appendix	46
XVI.	Bibliography	54

Forward

I'm not quite sure how to take mere words and put them together to adequately explain the impact that Betty has had on millions of people through her education of and advocacy for children, as well as presenting seminars and sharing her message of love and hope. Betty has her roots in education as a public school teacher and administrator, and as an owner/director of a Learning Center. I feel Betty is a master teacher and a dynamic administrator. She believes the ultimate goal of teaching is to have individuals strive for continuing self-growth and development. Her success is due to a value system in which she is a servant to others because she has a strong desire to help other people. She encourages others to seek their own higher priorities and to become servants themselves.

Betty believes that when children know their teachers and develop a trusting and safe relationship with them, then the children will learn more, learn it more easily, retain it longer and apply it more appropriately. This marks the combination of ideal and practical, which is what every teacher should strive for.

Adilia Frazer, Training Coordinator
Brazos Valley Child Care Management Services
Bryan, Texas

Introduction

This book is about different ways and appropriate words we can use to guide children and help them learn to control themselves. These words, methods, and ideas are effective ways to build self-esteem and make children feel good about themselves. They can be used to help teachers, parents, or anyone that works with children.

When my brothers, sisters and I were growing up, we just loved the joy and excitement our daddy shared with us. It seemed that he always knew the right thing to say to console us. As I got older one of my jobs was to baby-sit. Since my daddy had a special way with children, especially with infants, I often asked for his advice. He told me that when children were upset or wanted something they did not need, the best way to deal with them was to show them something else or do something to get their attention, like singing or just acting silly. Back then, my daddy said it was fooling the child into doing things that you wanted him or her to do. Today we call it redirecting. My mother was even wiser about child rearing. She told me that if you took really good care of babies by keeping them dry, warm and fed, they would sleep well, and be happy and cheery. Today we call it taking care of children's basic needs. Just like the old saying, all I need in life I learned in kindergarten, all that I know about basic infant and childcare, I learned from two of the wisest people I know; my mom and dad. I followed their advice concerning children during my baby-sitting career, and I used it in raising my own children, and during the many years I've taught other people's children.

After raising my own children and continuing to learn about what children do and why they do it, I am convinced that how you treat children, the words you use with them, and the guidance techniques you use make a great difference in their lives.

It takes a lot of patience and self-control to work with children. I view discipline as a means of teaching children. Children need discipline. In fact, children want you to set limits. Children aren't born knowing how to behave. It is up to adults to teach them. Consistency and following through is the key to improved behavior.

Research has proven that instruction through demonstration and modeling helps a child build self-esteem and confidence. On the other hand, research also shows that when children are continually reminded of what they are doing wrong, they feel worthless and defeated.

The techniques presented in this book are designed to help you to be a calm, confident teacher or parent so that your children will be encouraged, inspired and well rounded.

DISCIPLINE

Discipline

Webster's Dictionary defines discipline as "training which corrects, molds, or perfects the mental faculties or moral character." The root word of discipline means to teach, train or educate. Discipline is <u>not</u> punishment, but guidance.

Positive guidance is a particular technique used to discipline children. This teaching process involves methods that result in more successful behavior. It encourages the children to become more responsible and it gives them more options to improve their behavior. The positive guidance process is a challenge. It is more difficult and more time consuming, but the end result is learned behavior for life.

Punishment only temporarily stops bad behavior. It does not promote self-discipline. Madelyn Swift states that, "Punishment is something negative we do to children such as hurting them physically or emotionally to improve behavior. It creates resentment. You and your words no longer count with children." Punishment is easy, but it does not correct unwanted behavior. It is just a quick fix for the moment. All options are closed. The behavior learned by the child is to hurt, humiliate, shame and bully.

Early childhood educators know that children learn best through experience. Children must be redirected and guided lovingly to help them learn to cooperate. They must have positive educational experiences that encourage and enhance their growth and development.

One of the positive discipline tools my husband and I used in raising our children was a reward system. If they followed the rules, completed all their chores and did good in school we would reward their efforts. We posted a chart on which they could put a star each time chores were done correctly. Once they reached a specified number of stars on the chart they received a reward. For times when they did not follow the rules we would remind them what needed to be done and then count to three. This gave them time to think about what they needed to correct and how, then correct it, or start correcting, before we got to the number three. As they grew older, privileges such as shopping, going out with friends and later bedtime curfews were given as rewards.

WHY CHILDREN MISBEHAVE

Why Children Misbehave

There are many reasons children misbehave. Usually children misbehave because their needs are not being met. The environment must be set up appropriately according to the age of the children.

- There must be enough toys for all the children, preferably two of every toy.
- Classrooms should be arranged in a manner that encourages children to use good behavior.
- The schedule and play space should accommodate children's needs in a positive manner.

Here are some reasons that Clare Sherry and other researchers say children misbehave.

For example:

<u>INFANTS CRY AND FRET BECAUSE THEY:</u>
- are hungry
- are tired
- are teething
- are wet
- are sleepy
- do not want to interact with others
- lack trust
- are in an unpleasant environment

TODDLERS MISBEHAVE BECAUSE THEY:

- want attention
- are scared
- don't know an appropriate way to get what they want
- are tired
- are sleepy
- have too many "no-no's" in the environment
- are expected to wait too long
- have a limited, closed environment

PRESCHOOLERS MISBEHAVE BECAUSE THEY:

- are bored, there's not enough to do
- are testing the environment
- are not getting enough sleep
- are allergic to some foods
- are releasing stress and frustration
- are angry
- are expected to sit too long
- are expected to do things that are too complicated
- are expected to behave appropriately without guidance or role models
- are in a boring environment
- are not eating a proper diet

SCHOOLAGERS MISBEHAVE BECAUSE THEY:

- △ are testing the limits
- △ are seeking attention
- △ are frustrated and upset
- △ are asserting themselves and their independence
- △ have a lack of knowledge and experience
- △ have a lack of confidence

SOME SUGGESTED STRATEGIES FOR PREVENTING MISBEHAVIOR

Some Suggested Strategies for Preventing Misbehavior

These are some strategies that might help to prevent children from misbehaving:

- Try to understand the child's feelings and help him or her to express those feelings.
- When good behavior is exhibited, praise the child.
- Set expectations that the child can clearly understand.
- Before trouble begins, remove the child from the problem area.
- Provide a safe and stimulating environment.
- Give limited choices that are feasible.
- Have an easy flow from one activity to another.
- Make sure the child knows what's going to happen next.
- Give reasonable limitations to protect property and other children.
- Teach peaceful ways to solve conflicts.

POSITIVE GUIDANCE APPROACH

Positive Guidance Approach

INFANTS (0-12 MOS.)

Rima Shore says that "the first three years of life are essential to the development of basic trust. Infants need to be lovingly nurtured and cared for in order to foster trust." They need to be talked to while being fed and while having their diapers changed. When talking to infants, use real words. They need to learn that their environment is a good and safe place, and this idea as well as initial discipline can only be achieved through language and modeling.

The environment for the infant is an exploring field. Everything is for chewing, so check closely each morning and remove all/any objects from the floor. Infants must be supervised at all times. They are never to be left alone. You should stand or sit where you can see all the babies at any time. Make sure you acknowledge them by calling their names and talking to them about what they are looking at or what they are doing. For example, when you are bottle-feeding an infant talk to her about the feeding, and at the same time make conversation with the others by calling to them and saying, "Tashara, I see you swinging; you are going back and forth. Oh, what fun."

When you are changing an infant's diaper, make sure you have all the supplies at your fingertips. Never leave the infant on the changing table to get supplies. Always keep one hand on the child. Include other babies in conversation while you are at the changing table. Sing a song or say a rhyme with the infants' names in it. When an infant cries, respond quickly to her needs. Check the diapers and keep them dry. Feed the infants when they are hungry. Talk, sing, read or do finger plays with them. Hold the infant on your lap while you are reading a book.

When the infants begin teething, their gums get irritated and itch. To help with this, supply teething rings, hard bread sticks, or rub the baby's gums with a teether. Sometimes children will reach over and chew/bite another child to get relief from the pain. If the infant bites another, get down on the level of the biter, look the biter in the eye and say, "No, no you cannot bite, Lloyd." Comfort the victim, but keep your eyes on the biter to stop this from happening again. The preventive method is to supply chewing objects to an infant who is teething, but if this does not work, be sure to correct the child in a frim but calm voice. Then offer the biter a teething ring to promote proper behavior.

TODDLERS (12-23 MOS.)

Toddlers are limited in expressing themselves, although they do understand a great deal of language. Adults need to teach the toddlers what to say. When a toddler bites another toddler, it may be a carry over from a habit that was related to teething. Biting is usually not done to hurt someone; do as you did with the infants. Get on the toddler's level, say, "No, no," then turn away to the victim and tell the victim to say no to the toddler who bit him. Give the biter a teether to chew on or something to eat.

Guide the toddlers in a positive way. Toddlers need to play and move around. They should sit for only short periods of time. The rule of thumb is they should sit the length of time equal to their age, so about one to two minutes. Never force toddlers to just sit.

Toddlers should be given the opportunity to select their own toys, objects, and materials for play. The teacher should be a good role model and provide encouraging words. Talk about things the toddlers see and what they are doing. They may need help initiating an activity or expressing themselves. Correcting any behavior can be a learning opportunity for the child, and by using positive language and demonstrating appropriate behavior the teacher can help the child understand guidelines and follow them.

OLDER TODDLERS (24-35 MONTHS)

In the early stages of socialization, toddlers need the words to express their feelings. They get these from adults. Example, "RoShunda, I see you feel frustrated because you can't get the ball. Betty is playing with it. She will let you play with it when she is finished. Let's go play in the home center." This is redirecting. Offering the child another activity prevents conflict. Try to have two of each toy so toddlers will not be forced to share. At this age children are not ready to share. If they touch or have anything they feel it is theirs. They'll need a little time and help to develop a sense of sharing.

Biting is a natural behavior for young children. They bite and chew to relieve the pain that comes from teething. Biting during the early years is probably unrelated to anger or hostility, yet it must be corrected. Talk to the toddler on her eye level and say, "No biting. Biting hurts." Then turn to the victim and tell the victim to say, "No, it hurts." Give the biter a teether to chew on or something to eat.

Give the toddler the appropriate words to use whenever unacceptable behavior occurs. When a victim is involved, tell the victim to let the other toddler know that he or she doesn't like it. For example, if a toddler pinches another child, correct the pincher by saying, "No, we don't pinch. It hurts Linda when you pinch her." Then tell Linda the words to say to the pincher; "No, it hurts." In the conflict solution section of this book there are examples of methods and words that older toddlers may use to let other playmates know they don't like something. Give them the words to express themselves.

PRESCHOOLERS (3 – 5 YEARS)

Preschoolers can understand language and use it to express themselves. They need to have their feelings acknowledged, accepted, and respected. If the child is angry or upset, say, "Deborah, I see you are upset. It is really all right to be upset, but you are not to kick Johnny. Use your words." Always focus on the behavior, not on the child.

If a child is hurting, hitting, biting, kicking, or scratching another child, talk to the child in a low calm voice. Say, "Tonya, I know you

Positive Guidance Approach

are angry, but I cannot let you hurt anyone. When you are ready, we can talk about what you can do." Talk to the child about things she can do when she gets angry, such as tear up a bag or rags, pound a big ball of clay or go to a renewal area where she can play with soft huggable toys. A renewal area is used to help children regain control of themselves. When a child needs some time away from the group to calm down, the renewal area is where the child can go for a short while. Later, the teacher and child will discuss the problem and the child can give the solution of how she will solve the problem. Any time a child makes a little effort or some progress, acknowledge it by saying to the child, "Rachel, you've really tried to control yourself." Always focus on the behavior, and not the child.

Preschoolers, especially 3-year-olds, whine to express their feelings. You should say, "I can't understand you when you make crying noises." Look the child in the eyes and say, "Do you need something? Are you tired? Do you need a hug?" Whining is a clue that the child needs you. Help the child communicate what he or she needs.

SCHOOLAGERS (6 – 12 YEARS)

Schoolagers are more independent and can use age appropriate self-help skills, such as personal grooming, caring for materials and solving problems. Focus for schoolagers should be on how to develop self-discipline and become become responsible. The teacher should be a positive role model for the children. The teacher and children should treat one another with dignity and respect at all times. Let the children help set the rules and consequences. The teacher and students can create a behavior chart, which is signed by the children and posted on the wall. When a child doesn't follow a rule the teacher refers to the chart, shows the child his signature and has the child review the rules. When rules are followed, when extra special activities and chores are done or children make excellent grades, the teacher can allow them to place their name in a basket. A child's name can go in the basket more than one time. At the end of the week draw several names from the basket and allow those children to pick a treat or prize from a goody box. This type of reward system helps make children motivated and accountable for good behavior.

Schoolagers learn best when they are loved and supported. Nurture them and expect the best from them. Children live up to adults' expectations. Use problem-solving strategies to identify the causes of misbehavior; this also helps involve the children and allows them to learn something they can apply later.

When schoolagers are not getting along with each other, are calling each other names or have any conflicts, this is a time to use problem solving strategies. Have an area set up with a small table where the rules are posted. Seat the children on opposite sides of the table facing each other. If it is a heated problem like fighting or hurting someone, a mediator such as the teacher should be present. The children should discuss the rules and how they can solve the problem by following the steps to a mutual solution.

PROBLEM SOLVING STRATEGIES

When setting up the rules and limitations be sure to provide some means of controlling the problem solving process. Decide to use a timer, teacher's whistle, or other 2-minute warning systems.

SOME RULES TO FOLLOW DURING THE PROBLEM SOLVING SESSION ARE:

1. Each person has a turn to tell what happened while everyone involved listens.

2. Each person can tell what they could have done differently to prevent the problem.

3. Everyone agrees on a solution to the problem and abides by the solution.

4. Each person's final comments are to say thanks, forgive and think about what technique they could or would use the next time a problem arises.

Positive Guidance Approach

WHAT TEACHERS CAN DO

What Teachers Can Do

Teachers play a vital role in the life of a child. Statistics say the average child spends a third of his day in school. After parents, teachers are the major resource in molding the minds of children and preparing them to become successful. Children look to adults as role models for what is appropriate. They imitate adults. It is the adult's responsibility to create the atmosphere and provide the models that enable the young child to develop self-control. Remember children want to please; they want to live up to your expectations

Discipline children positively:

- Show respect by seeking meaningful conversation with children.
- Use patience rather than force by encouraging appropriate behavior.
- Prepare and plan ahead by having everything ready when the children arrive.
- Be polite and honest by speaking kind words and telling the truth.
- Listen to children with attention and respect.
- Be consistent by following a daily schedule.
- Give children plenty of advance notice before changing activities.
- Interact with the child by smiling at him/her.
- Touch the child on the shoulder to get his attention or calm him/her.
- Hold a child closely to comfort and reassure him/her.
- Set clear, consistent and fair limits.
- Remove a child from the group when he/she needs renewal time.
- Be sensible and fair by applying the same rules to all.
- Be firm yet gentle in applying consequences.

- Be patient and allow children plenty of time.
- Give children words to use when there is a conflict and model appropriate responses.
- Help children learn appropriate social skills by encouraging cooperation and taking turns.
- Encourage and support children's efforts.
- Say, "I like you;" this lifts a child's self-esteem.
- Give children choices and allow them to make decisions.
- Model polite words such as, "Please" and "Thank you!"
- Give a back rub to calm a child who is upset or uncomfortable.
- Read stories to children.
- Use positive language with the children by avoiding "no" words.
- Let the children see you feel good about yourself by smiling and joining in their play.
- Discuss mistakes with children to help them reach a solution.
- Emphasize the positive things children do each day.
- Find ways to let each child know he/she is special.
- Hug each child to express love and acceptance.
- Help children understand their own feelings by listening and acknowledging their frustrations.
- Take children's feelings and thoughts seriously and let the child know it is all right to be upset.
- Give plenty of encouragement when the child is making progress.
- Always focus on the behavior and not the child.

What Teachers Can Do

ENCOURAGE PROBLEM-SOLVING:

- When reading a story stop and ask, "What do you think will happen next?" This gives children a chance to predict what will happen.

- When doing a finger play ask, "What new ways can we move our fingers?" This gives children the chance to use their own ideas instead of just memorizing the finger play.

- When outside on a walk ask, "Where do you think those clouds are going?" This helps children think about the world without worrying about right or wrong answers.

- When out on the playground ask, "What games can four children play with one ball?" This helps children think of ways to play and cooperate with each other.

- When passing by the house play area ask, "What are you cooking today? How did you make that?" This helps children expand their play and stretch their imaginations.

- When playing in the block play area ask, "How did you know to put the car at the top of the ramp to make it roll?" This helps children think about what they have learned from their experiences.

- When looking at a picture book about cars ask, "What would happen if all the cars stopped working?" This helps children use their imagination in new ways.

- When talking about yesterdays' walk in the woods ask, "What are some things you remember about the woods?" This helps children recall their experiences.

- Offer plenty of practice in problem solving with puzzles, games, and riddles.

- Observe children in problem-solving situations. Your presence and attention as they work is an important source of support to young children.

AVOID POWER STRUGGLES:

- Have a positive place to redirect children. "Would it help if you went to the pillows for awhile?"

- Never single out one child as contributing to the problem.

- Hugs make children feel accepted, valued, loved, and respected!!!

NONVERBAL TECHNIQUES:

- Stare at the child.
- Clear your throat.
- Shake your head.
- Use sign language.

Using these techniques and approaches to discipline children is not always easy for teachers or parents. It takes patience and caring to work with children who may be sick, hungry, angry, frustrated or just tired. It is the adult's responsibility to stay calm. If a group area becomes a problem, say, "I see you are having difficulty in this area. This area is now closed." Redirect the children to other activities. Say, "Each of you will now choose another activity in the room. No two will go to the same activity."

When I taught in public school I used many of these techniques with children that were labeled as problem students. When a problem child was coming into my class I would ask other teachers questions about the child. I would talk to friends of the child to find out things. When the child came to my class I would try to keep him busy with little projects and chores. I would allow the child to be responsible for passing out papers, cleaning the blackboard or taking care of the class pet. I would keep the child busy so there was no time for distractions. I would allow the child seven minutes each day to come to my desk and the two of us could talk about things. I tried to keep the conversation light and cheerful to ease stress from the child's day. This quality time made the child feel important and special. I also tried to do activities outside of the classroom with the child. I would take the child to a museum, skating or bowling, or to a pizza party. Whatever activity we did I tried to make it a learning experience for the child. Just giving a child a little extra attention and care can mean a world of difference in their attitude and personality.

TEACHER'S RESPONSIBILITY FOR DISCIPLINE

Teachers' Responsibility for Discipline

- Have a positive attitude regarding behavior. If you expect children to behave, they will.

- Be consistent about what is acceptable and what is not acceptable.

- Set an example for children. If you shout, refuse to listen, hit or grab things out of their hands, children see this as the way to solve problems.

- Know the abilities, attention span, and needs of the children you teach. Know what are reasonable expectations for your age group.

- Alternate quiet and active play when planning the daily schedule.

- Arrange play space so children are not crowded, but avoid big open spaces that invite running and chasing.

- Allow time to give each child some individual attention.

- Maintain a sense of humor and enjoy the children.

WHAT CHILDREN SHOULD KNOW

What Children Should Know

Children are constantly learning and sorting out things. They may hear what you say, but not know what you mean. If you say, "Don't run," they may hear run and think that they should run. It is more effective, and children can process language better, if we tell them what to expect. For example, if a child is running inside say, "Sharon, remember we walk inside." Then have the child repeat the rule and model the correct behavior.

Children should also know what is going to happen next. Be consistent with daily scheduling and routine. For example, say, "Boys and girls we will put everything back in place so we can go to lunch." If a child says, "I want to go outside to play," the response might be, "Morgan, we will pick up the toys, go to lunch and then we will go outside." At home it is important to have a regular schedule for children. When your child comes home from school remind him or her of the routine: change clothes, eat a snack, do homework, have someone review homework, 10 minute break, do chores and then go outside and play. Post a daily schedule for the child so that he/she can refer to it.

HELPING CHILDREN FIND THEIR OWN SOLUTIONS

- ○ Provide an environment with stimulating and challenging materials and activities.
- ○ Give each child some one-on-one time every day.
- ○ Model appropriate use of material.
- ○ Reinforce positive behavior whenever possible.
- ○ Observe closely as children explore to see what they understand.
- ○ Pose additional challenges to further expand children's thinking.
- ○ Be firm. Being firm doesn't mean being harsh or loud. Use a calm, but gentle and firm voice.

WHAT PARENTS CAN DO

What Parents Can Do

Parents are their child's first teachers. Set aside quality time with your child on a daily basis. Your role is vital if positive guidance and self-discipline are to be successful. Parents have the most influence over a child's early learning years and positive parental interaction helps determine success in later years.

- Be a role model for your child.
- Take time out for your child.
- Read to your child.
- Talk and listen to your child.
- Ask your child about his/her day.
- Give your child words to express feelings and emotions.
- Assure your child you love him/her.
- Be consistent.
- Be patient.
- Make sure your child eats nourishing meals.
- Conference with your child's teacher.
- Get involved at your child's center or school.
- Balance active play with rest time.

Several parents approached me about the techniques I used to raise my children. I was told that my children were well mannered and appeared to make good choices. These are the steps that I shared with them.

When the children were infants we took care of their basic needs. We did it in a pleasurable loving way. We made sure we were relaxed and free of stress and hurrying. We talked to the babies about what we were doing. We played and laughed with them. We had a time set aside that we read to them each day. As the children grew up we encouraged them to tell us what they thought or wanted and we listened attentively, by giving our total focus to the children.

I feel children should be acknowledged, respected and treated with kindness. We shouldn't hurry and use unpleasant voices with children. Prepare ahead of time to prevent rushing and stress.

Be consistent; if it is wrong today it is still wrong tomorrow. If it is not an appropriate thing for children to do, then don't allow it today or tomorrow. Do not give children mixed signals. They are learning and they get confused. Confusion may cause fretting, aggression, and misbehavior.

During the toddler and later years we always tried to give two choices. When they made good choices we acknowledged and praised them. This reinforced the behavior and life style we wanted. When a bad choice was made we talked about the choice, what happened and why. The consequence was applied and the children learned the correct choice to make the next time.

We let the children know they could talk to us about anything that was of concern and interesting to them. This helped us to develop open communication. We also told them that we were never too busy to listen or to help them. We meant it and we kept our word. The children tried it and we followed through with what we had promised.

One evening one of the children came into my room to get help with her homework. Her daddy came by and said, "RoShunda, come out of your mother's room, she is not feeling well." RoShunda looked at her daddy and said "Daddy, momma said she is never too sick or tired to help me." Children take us at our word and when we fail in keeping our promise it causes the children to doubt and stop trusting us. I helped her even though I didn't feel well and this maintained our trust. My husband would pick up the children from school most evenings. The minute they got into the truck, they would start talking to their dad about what they did, needed and wanted to do. We taught our children to know that there are some things you don't get just because you ask. When they ask for things that we as parents don't think are safe or appropriate for them, then we have to make choices too. We have to make the best choice for them and explain it as well.

One day Tashara came home from school a little upset. She said, "Momma, the teacher had the whole class write 50 sentences of 'I will not talk out and act out in class'. I don't think it is fair." I asked her what happened for the teacher to have everyone write sentences. Tashara said, "When the teacher walked into the room most of the children were up out of their seats screaming and hollering." I asked her, "Do you think the teacher could see who was doing the screaming and hollering?" She said she didn't think so. I told her the teacher probably couldn't see everybody and so she had to punish the whole group. I told her that it wasn't going to hurt her to write the sentences, and that she learned a good lesson. Everything in life is not fair, and sometimes we have to do things we don't like for the good of the group. On the other hand, however, there are times when you will have to go to the school on behalf of your child. During these times go with a calm attitude to resolve the problem for the child and the school. My daughter, Tanisha, came home with a paper that she felt was graded wrong. I checked the paper and agreed with Tanisha that there were some things on the paper marked incorrectly. I contacted the teacher at the school and set up a meeting. We went over Tanisha's paper and found that the teacher had erred in some of her grading. A correction was made and everybody was happy because the situation was dealt with calmly and politely.

At around the age of 6, we started using the "What should you have done to solve the problem" methods. It is similar to the conflict resolution procedure. We got more into problem solving and responsibility about 10 years of age. It wasn't long before my children became more independent in solving their conflicts and my husband and I didn't get involved as much. We noticed and observed from afar. We only stepped in when it was absolutely necessary.

These were consequences for when good choices were not made. Some of the consequences we used were:

▼ Loss of movie day

▼ Loss of driving privileges

▼ No TV watching

▼ No going out to park or group activities with friends

▼ Early curfew

▼ Loss of telephone time

Beginning in the pre-teen years we had monthly family meetings. We would gather to discuss topics and what information we deemed necessary. For 20-30 minutes we talked about the do's and don'ts, the what and why in different situations. The children came to understand that the success you have comes from the choices you make.

WE USED TOPICS AND SCENARIOS SUCH AS:

- ○ What should you do if someone offers you drugs? Why?
- ○ We watched special movies together and discussed the meaning.

One year we watched a Bill Cosby show where the children had the responsibility of taking care of animals as if they were parents. When the child had to go to the store, he had to take the baby with him. When he was going out with friends, he had to get a baby sitter. This show was used to deter young children from the serious mistake of becoming parents too early.

SCHOOL PROJECTS COULD BE A SOURCE OF DISCUSSION.

My daughter, Tashara, had a class project where they experimented with parenting skills. She brought home a plastic doll, Baby Think It Over, that she had to keep as if it were her own child. When she would come home she would try to go places and leave the doll at home. I made her follow through with the project and take the doll with her everywhere. When the family went out to eat, Tashara had to take the doll and hold it while she was eating. If she went to the mall she had to take the doll with her.

This experience reinforced what we had learned from the Bill Cosby show. Discussion of real life experiences gave our children the tools they needed to make wise choices when they were older.

GUIDING CHILDREN IN SOLVING CONFLICTS

Guiding Children in Solving Conflicts

Conflict resolution is a process to help children work through and solve problems. It teaches children how to make good choices and it helps a child find the appropriate words to express feelings. When you discipline a child, go to the child and kneel down at the child's eye level. If a child strikes the teacher, restrain the child gently, look the child in the eyes and say, "I don't like to be hit." Remember children are all different. What works for one may not work for another. You may need to try different techniques. Some children need more time, patience, consistency and firmness. All children need words to use to solve a conflict.

WHAT TEACHERS AND PARENTS CAN DO TO HELP CHILDREN SOLVE CONFLICTS

- When a child takes play dough from another child say, "How about using it together? You can have some and she can have some."

- When a child pulls another child off the tricycle say, "Clinton, let Lloyd finish his turn. Then you can have a turn. That way you both get a turn. Clinton, when I count to three it is Lloyd's turn." Count as slow or as fast as needed, then say, "It's Lloyd's turn now, Clinton."

- When a child pushes another child say, "Sue, I see you want to have the grocery basket, but you may not push Karen out of the way to get it. Use your words. Ask Karen if you may have a turn. If she says yes, you can have a turn. If she says no, then you must wait for your turn and choose to work at another center until she finishes."

- When a child is upset because no one will play with her or him say, "Missy, it's okay to want to play with Leigha, but you feel a little sad when she says no. It is not okay to hit her. You can play by yourself or ask someone else to play with you. I'll play with you."

- When a child paints on another child's picture say, "Tashara you may paint a picture on your own paper. I can't let you paint on RoShunda's paper. Come, let's get RoShunda another piece of paper and you can have a piece."

- When a child is having a hard time waiting for a turn say, "Charla, I know it seems that you have been waiting a long time to play at the sand table. You are getting tired of waiting so you are screaming. You can tell Jenny you've been waiting a long time and want your turn, or you could work at another center until Jenny finishes. The time goes faster then."

- When a child destroys things say, "Matt, you may not hit the furniture with the hammer. If you want to pound something, you may go to the wood working table." Provide a place where the child can pound, make a mess, cut and tear. Teach them what they may and may not do.

- When a child uses bad language, stay calm. Don't act excited or shocked. Don't scold, punish or over emphasize it. Merely relax and say, "That word is not a word we use. Let's try rhyming some words." Sometimes it is best just to ignore it. If the bad language continues, bring it to the parents' attention with suggestions of how to handle it.

- When a child grabs another child's toy and runs away, say, "Jose, tell Wesley that he is not to take the toy from you.

If he wants to play with it, Wesley must use his words and ask you if he can play with the toy when you finish."

- When a child fills his hand with sand and throws it at other children say, "Wazzie, keep the sand in the sand table. It's not for throwing on anyone. If you want something to throw, get a ball to throw outside."

- When a child screams because there isn't enough of one kind of toy say, "Derrick, it's okay to want the toy, but Juan is playing with it now. Screaming doesn't help you get the toy. You need to use your words. Ask Juan if you can play with the toy. Let's see what else you can play with until Juan finishes."

- When a child throws things say, "Deborah, blocks are for stacking and building. You may throw the ball when we go outside."

HELPING CHILDREN TO SOLVE THEIR OWN CONFLICTS

- Guide children in solving their own problems. Give them appropriate words to use.

- Enable children to reach their own solutions by modeling proper responses to problems.

- Allow children to have a safe outlet to express his/her feelings; i.e. a pillow for hitting or a teddy bear to hug.

- Provide children a renewal area where they can freely discuss problems and learn to make better choices.

DISCIPLINE METHODS

Discipline Methods

NEGATIVE METHODS TO AVOID

Try as much as possible to eliminate the words "no", "don't", "can't", "bad", etc. from your vocabulary. Remember that negative words are dead words.

Examples of Negative Methods to avoid:

▼ <u>No</u>, you are not going to play over there.

▼ <u>No</u>, you are not going to recess!

▼ <u>Don't</u> you dare!

▼ <u>Stop</u> hitting him!

▼ <u>No</u>, you may <u>not</u>!

▼ <u>You are not</u> going to act like that in here.

▼ <u>You can't</u> have your way. I'm the teacher (parent).

When discussing negative behavior with a child it is best to avoid repeating all the details of what happened. Tell the child <u>what to do</u> instead of <u>what just happened</u>. If you must use negative words (hit, run, bite, can't, don't), always say something positive before you use them.

Examples of Positive Methods to Use:

▲ <u>We will</u> walk inside. You may run when we go outside.

▲ <u>I like</u> the colors you use.

▲ <u>Are you</u> forgetting to take turns?

▲ <u>Use</u> quiet voices inside.

▲ <u>We build</u> with blocks on the floor.

▲ <u>You will</u> feel better if you rest a minute.

▲ <u>I need</u> your help. Can you help me?

PREVENTIVE METHOD

The best prevention for inappropriate behavior is to be well prepared and plan for times that might cause a problem. When there are situations where you anticipate that a child may have a problem, it is best to keep the child near you. Hold the child's hand or have the child sit next to you during circle time. Plan ahead and be prepared. Being prepared is the key to successful guidance. Check the classroom to see if any particular areas cause or bring on inappropriate behavior. Make adjustments to prevent the behavior from being repeated.

According to the Early Childhood Educators Outcome, a good opportunity to help children learn is wasted if a child is punished when an explanation might eliminate the inappropriate behavior. You should help children to understand that while a certain behavior is unacceptable, they are always valued. When redirecting or correcting children's behavior, the law forbids any form of hitting, corporal punishment, abusive language, ridicule or harsh, humiliating or frightening treatment of children.

FIRMER METHOD

This method comes just before the team method. It occurs in three steps. If step one doesn't work, go to step two and so on.

<u>Step 1:</u>   Change your tone of voice to be firm, yet calm. Make your voice sound more serious, indicating that you actually mean what you say. Example: "Tony sit down!"

<u>Step 2:</u>   State firmly what you want the child to do. Example: "Tony sit down!!"

<u>Step 3:</u>   Get firmer by stating in a stern voice and adding the word "now". Example: "Tony, sit down now!!!"

TEAM METHOD

It is important that the childcare center or school and home be on the same team in using positive guidance. Parents should be informed of what positive guidance techniques are being used and encouraged to use the same at home. When a child's behavior is inappropriate, the teacher should conference with the parent to discuss what means of correction have and have not been successful. Include the center director or principal in seeking more help, if it is needed. An outside resource agency may also need to be called for assistance. Such agencies as Child Protective Services, child advocacy agencies, mediation agencies, and local juvenile service counselors, as well as school counselors, community counselors, church clergy and local psychologists can provide information and help in positive guidance skills.

LAST RESORT

If there is still a problem after exhausting the positive guidance technique or the team method, you may need a stronger course of action.

The Burn Out Behavior Technique allows the child to repeat the behavior over and over until he/she tires of it. The adult stops the repeated behavior and has the child say it will not happen again.

If every day the teacher sends home a behavior note, and if the teacher and parent have worked together on all of the aforementioned methods and nothing seems to help, then try the Burn Out Technique.

EXAMPLES:

Children are fighting in school. Take the two children aside and set them face-to-face but not close enough to touch. Tell them to punch at the air repeatedly. After so long the children will tire of punching at the air. Tell them every time they fight they will have to do this. They soon grow tired and don't want to fight.

If a child runs inside repeatedly when told not to, take the child outside and let them run repeatedly back and forth in a certain area until they tire.

If a child throws a toy instead putting it back in place properly, set the child aside and give the child a soft stuffed toy and a basket. Let the child throw the toy into the basket repeatedly until he tires of it.

KEYS TO
POSITIVE
DISCIPLINE

Keys to Positive Discipline

IMPORTANT KEYS FOR DISCIPLINE WITH LOVE

- Emphasize the positive things children do.
- Help children understand their own feelings.
- Help children learn appropriate social skills.
- Give children choices whenever possible.
- Be consistent.
- Listen to children.
- Keep a problem child close to you.
- Let children become part of the story, finger play or song by using their names.
- Help children find the solution to problems.

CONCLUSION

Conclusion

Use each difficult time as a teaching moment. We needn't get excited about every little fight, scratch and bump. However, when children repeat a behavior over and over and it results in injury to another, we must accept the fact that they may deliberately intend to hurt. If it appears that children deliberately intend to hurt one another, then the parent or teacher should intervene. Tell the child doing the hurting that you can't allow her or him to hurt anyone. If it happens again he/she will lose privileges and/or will have to sit out for a time. It is important that "sit out time" be appropriate to a child's age, i.e. 1 minute for 1 year olds, 2 minutes for 2 year olds, etc.

It is the adult's responsibility to be a good role model, give choices, respect a child's needs, and reinforce positive behavior.

Every child is unique and special. They are God's gift. I believe the saying, "Every child can learn." Help the child to be proud of him or herself. Love and care for children and be sincere. The children need us. They are our hope. Let us work together so they can be successful in life.

APPENDIX

Appendix

SOME SUGGESTED ACCEPTABLE GUIDANCE SAYINGS

Here are examples of appropriate responses that may be used to guide children.

If this happens:	Say:
A child screams because there isn't enough of one kind of toy.	"Vonda, it's okay to want to have your own shovel like the other children, but screaming doesn't help you get a shovel. You need to use your words. Ask if anyone is ready to give you his or her shovel, or let's see what else you can dig with."
A child is upset because a friend won't play.	"Domonique, it's okay to want to play with Kent. You feel a little sad when he says no. It's not okay to hit him when he wants to play alone. You can play by yourself on the jungle gym, or ask someone else to play with you."
A child hits another child.	"Tiawanna, I know you feel like hitting Nancy, but it hurts when we use our hands the wrong way."

If this happens:	Say:
A child leaves the water running.	"Candi, so we don't waste water you need to turn the water off."
Children are pushing and pulling on the way to recess.	"Are we forgetting to take turns?"
A child is not cleaning up.	"Melissa, everyone needs to help. Your job is to throw the scraps in the trash can."
A child is running.	"Ethel, if you are running, you could fall. Remember to walk."
A child is crying.	"Carla, you're really feeling sad. Would you like to tell me why you're unhappy? Maybe I can help."
Children are yelling.	"Let's speak softly. Use your inside voice."
A child is throwing sand.	"Xaiver, when sand is thrown, it gets into our eyes. You may play in the sandbox without throwing sand, or you may play on the slide. Which do you choose?"
A child is pushing other children on the slide.	"Jamie, it's dangerous to push people on the slide. They may get hurt."

If this happens:	Say:
A child's time is up.	"Uchenna, you need to finish up because Chung has been waiting a long time for her turn."
A child is talking very loud.	"Please use quiet voices inside. Save loud voices for outside."
A child is swinging a stick around	"Please put the stick down so no one will get hurt."
A child pushes another child.	"Carlos, you want to wheel the doll carriage, but you may not push Mary out of the way. She was already wheeling the carriage. Ask Mary if you can have a turn. If she says yes, you can have the carriage. If she says no, you must wait your turn."
A child takes play dough from another child.	"You may have some of your own play dough. You may not take Mike's dough from him. Why don't you use it together? You can have some and he can have some. Ask Mike to share his play dough or ask me for some."
A child is having a hard time waiting for a turn.	"Raquel, you have waited a long time for the trike. You are getting tired of waiting so you are calling Tonja crazy. You may not call her crazy. She is not crazy and neither are you. You can tell Tonja that you have waited a long time and want a turn now."

Appendix

If this happens:	**Say:**
A child is acting up.	"I love you, but I do not like the way you are acting. Are you making good choices?"
A child is working on a difficult task.	"This is not easy to learn. We will work on it at another time. I will help you."
A child won't share.	"Joycelyn likes it too. It would be nice to share with her."
A child gets hurt.	"Come, I'll kiss it," or "Come, let me hold you until it stops hurting."
A child is not putting things away.	"Wazzie, the blocks are on the floor. Please pick them up. Come, I'll help you. Thank you for helping me!"
A child is calling names.	"Dimple, he doesn't like it when you call him that. It hurts his feelings."
A child is not resting at nap time.	"Trey, you'll feel better if you rest a minute."
A child is pulling hair.	"James, it hurts when you pull Patty's hair. It makes her unhappy".
A child will not stop playing at the center during story time.	"Melvin would like to continue painting. He'll join us later."
Children are working together.	"I feel so happy, seeing all of you working happily together."

Appendix

If this happens:	Say:
Children are noisy.	"It's time to be quiet."
Children need to sit down.	"Let's sit down now."
The door needs to be closed.	"Please close the door, Melvin."
A child is spitting on other children.	"Tim, spitting spreads germs and others don't like it. If you are angry, we can talk about it."
A child is throwing a shovel.	"Please use the shovel to dig with. If you want to throw something, you can throw the ball outside."
A child is throwing blocks.	"We build with blocks on the floor."
A child is throwing blocks during clean-up time.	"Steve, let's see how neatly we can stack the blocks."
A child is dumping puzzle pieces on the floor.	"Byron, it's better to take pieces out one at a time."
A child needs help finishing a puzzle.	"Betty, if you need help, maybe Harry can help you put it back together."
A child is throwing a ball in the classroom.	"George, your ball needs to go on the shelf until playground time. I'd love to see how far you could throw when we are outdoors where nothing can break."
The home area is not clean.	"I need helpers to straighten the home area."

Appendix

If this happens:	Say:
A child colored all over his work.	"Tom, it looks like you had fun using all those colors."
A child is talking too much.	"Ming-Le, I'm glad you want to tell us about your trip, but you need to take turns listening."
A child is not sitting and listening.	"Jeffrey, I need to see your eyes. I like the way Mary is listening (or sitting)."
Paint is dripping on the floor.	"We press the brush inside the jar, like this."
A child is climbing on the bookshelf.	"Kathy, are you making a good choice?"
A child is kicking.	"We use our feet for walking."
A child is spitting or biting.	"We use our mouth to chew food."
A child is tearing up things.	"Books are to look at and puzzles are to be put together."
A child is acting up.	"I am disappointed. I depend on you to do better. If it happens again, you will have to go to another center."

BIBLIOGRAPHY

Bibliography

Bowdoin, Ruth. *"Words That Win Children."* Nashville, Tennessee: Webster's International Tutoring Systems, Inc., 1976.

Bowdoin, Ruth. *"Parents are Teachers."* Nashville, Tennessee: Webster's International Tutoring Systems, Inc., 1976.

Cherry, Clare. *"Please Don't Sit on the Kids: Alternatives to Punitive Discipline."* Carthage, Illinois: Fearon Teacher Aids, 1983.

Duffy, Roslyn. *"From a Parent's Perspective."* Child Care Information Exchange (1998): 29 – 30.

Fields, Margorie and Cindy Boesser. *"Constructive Guidance and Discipline."* Upper Saddle River, New Jersey: Prentice Hall, 1998.

Nelsen, Jane. *"Positive Discipline."* New York, New York: Ballantine Books, 1996.

Shore, Rima. *"Rethinking the Brain: New Insights Into Early Development."* New York, New York: Families and Work Institute, 1997.

Steffens, Pat, *"Why Children Misbehave."* Lincoln, Nebraska: Family Life (Nov. 1993 issue).

Stone, Jeannette Galambos. *"A Guide to Discipline."* Washington, D.C.: The National Association for the Education of Young Children, 1994.

Stone, Jeannette. *"Caregiver and Teacher Language; Responsive or Restrictive?"* Washington, D.C.: Young Children Journal of The National Association for the Education of Young Children (May 1993, Vol. 48): 12-18.

Swift, Madelyn. *"Discipline for Life: Getting it Right with Children."* Fort Worth, Texas: Stairway Education Programs, 1998.

Notes